Treasury Department—Bureau of Statistics.

SCHEDULE B.

CLASSIFICATION OF COMMODITIES, AND LAWS AND REGULATIONS GOVERNING THE PREPARATION

OF

MONTHLY STATEMENTS OF DOMESTIC EXPORTS.

APPROVED JUNE 15, 1900.

WASHINGTON:
GOVERNMENT PRINTING OFFICE.
1900.

In the interest of creating a more extensive selection of rare historical book reprints, we have chosen to reproduce this title even though it may possibly have occasional imperfections such as missing and blurred pages, missing text, poor pictures, markings, dark backgrounds and other reproduction issues beyond our control. Because this work is culturally important, we have made it available as a part of our commitment to protecting, preserving and promoting the world's literature. Thank you for your understanding.

SCHEDULE B.

Laws and Regulations governing the preparation of Monthly Statements of Domestic Exports.

TREASURY DEPARTMENT, *June 15, 1900.*

To collectors of customs and others:

1. Beginning with the first day of July, 1900, the annexed Schedule B will govern the classification of commodities, the growth, produce, or manufacture of the United States exported to foreign countries, in the monthly statements rendered by collectors of customs to the Bureau of Statistics of this Department. *This schedule supersedes all prior schedules for the classification of domestic exports.*

2. Attention is called to the provisions of law and customs regulations controlling the preparation of the statistical returns under this schedule.

LAW AND REGULATIONS AS TO EXPORTS IN VESSELS.

3. Before a clearance shall be granted for any vessel bound to a foreign place, the collector shall require the owners, shippers, or consignors of the cargo to deliver to the collector manifests of the cargo, or the parts thereof shipped by them respectively, which manifests shall specify the kinds and quantities of articles shipped by them respectively, and the value of the total quantity of each kind of articles; and state that such manifest contains a full, just, and true account of all articles laden on board of such vessel by the owners, shippers, or consignors, respectively, and that the values of such articles are truly stated, according to their actual cost, or the values which they truly bear at the port and time of exportation. And the collector shall also require the master of the vessel, and the owners, shippers, and consignors of the cargo to state in writing, to the collector, the foreign place or country in which such cargo is truly intended to be landed. The manifests and statements hereby required shall be verified by the oath of the person by whom they are respectively made and subscribed. (Rev. Stat., 337.)

4. The master or person having the charge or command of any vessel bound to a foreign port, shall deliver to the collector of the district from which such vessel is about to depart, a manifest of all the cargo on board the same, and the value thereof, by him subscribed, and shall swear to the truth thereof; whereupon the collector shall grant a clearance for such vessel and her cargo, but without specifying the particulars thereof in the clearance, unless required by the master or other person having the charge or command of such vessel so to do. If any vessel bound to

a foreign port departs on her voyage to such foreign port without delivering such manifest and obtaining a clearance as hereby required, the master or other person having the charge or command of such vessel shall be liable to a penalty of five hundred dollars for every such offense. (Rev. Stat., 4197.)

5. Agents of steamships, transportation companies, and others at points of shipment on the seaboard to whom is consigned merchandise on through bills of lading, or otherwise, from interior ports for export, should require the owner or shipper at the interior or initial point of shipment to accompany the merchandise with a list thereof or transmit by mail such list to the consignee or agent who is to clear the merchandise at the seaboard port for his information in preparing a proper manifest for the clearance of the goods. This list will show the kinds, quantities, values, and ultimate destination of the articles, inasmuch as the bills of lading do not contain sufficient information, especially with respect to manufactured articles, to enable the steamship agent or person charged with the preparation of the export manifest to intelligently comply with the law which requires such manifests to exhibit a full, just, and true account of the quantities and values of the merchandise exported at the port and time of exportation. (See arts. 1881 and 1882.)

LAW AND REGULATIONS AS TO EXPORTS BY LAND VEHICLES.

6. That hereafter collectors of customs shall render to the Bureau of Statistics, in such manner and form and at such periods as the Secretary of the Treasury may prescribe, returns of exports to foreign countries leaving the United States by rail. Any person who shall hereafter deliver to any railway or transportation company or other common carrier commodities for transportation and exportation by rail from the United States to foreign countries, shall also deliver to the collector of customs at the frontier port through which the goods pass into the foreign country a manifest, in such form as the Secretary of the Treasury may prescribe, duly certified as to its accuracy by said person or his agent, exhibiting the kinds, quantities, and values of the several articles delivered by such person or his agent for exportation. And no railway car containing commodities, the product or manufacture of the United States or foreign goods, duty paid or free of duty, intended to be exported to any foreign country, shall be permitted hereafter to leave the United States until the agent of the railway or transportation company, or the person having such car in charge, shall deliver to the customs officer at the last port in the United States through which the commodities pass into foreign territory a manifest thereof, which shall specify the kinds and quantities of the commodities in the form prescribed by the Secretary of the Treasury, and until the manifest, exhibiting the kinds, quantities, and values of the several commodities, shall have been delivered to the collector of customs, as above required, by the person exporting such commodities, or by his agent, or information [is furnished] satisfactory to such customs officer as to the kind, quanti-

ties, and values of the domestic and foreign free or duty-paid commodities laden on such car. The agent or employé of any railway or transportation company who shall transport such commodities into a foreign country before the delivery to the collector of customs of the manifest (s), as above required, shall be liable to a penalty of fifty dollars for each offense : *Provided*, That the provisions of this law shall apply to commodities transported to the frontier in railway cars for exportation and transshipment across the frontier into the adjacent foreign territory in ferryboats or vehicles, so far as to require the person in charge thereof to furnish to the collector of customs information of the kinds, quantities, and values of such commodities : *And provided further*, That nothing contained in the foregoing shall be held as applicable to goods in transit between American ports by routes passing through foreign territory or to merchandise in transit between places in the Dominion of Canada by routes passing through the United States, or to merchandise arriving at the ports designated under the authority of section three thousand and five of the Revised Statutes, and which may be destined for places in the Republic of Mexico. [Act March 3, 1893.]

7. The foregoing provision of law [paragraph 5] applies only to articles intended to be exported by land carriage or ferryboat to or through adjacent foreign territory for a market. It does not apply to articles shipped from one part of the United States to another part thereof across foreign territory, whether for exportation from the latter point or otherwise, nor to merchandise passing through the United States in transit from one foreign country to another, or from one portion of a foreign country to another portion thereof, across the territory of the United States. (Customs Regs., 1899, art. 1886.)

8. The list or manifest of articles to be exported, required to be furnished by the person exporting them or by his agent, to the collector of customs of the frontier customs district of the United States through which the articles are transported into the foreign country, shall be in the following form :

[Form 208, Customs Regs., 1899.]

OWNER'S OR AGENT'S MANIFEST OF ARTICLES EXPORTED BY RAILWAY.

List, or manifest, of articles of domestic production or manufacture, and of foreign articles, free of duty or duty paid, delivered by (name of owner or agent) to (name of railway or transportation company, station, and agent) for exportation to (place of intended destination in foreign country) via (name of last port in United States whence the articles pass into the foreign country).

Marks and numbers of packages.	Description of articles.	Domestic articles.		Foreign articles, free of duty or duty paid.	
		Quantities.	Values.	Quantities.	Values.
			Dollars.		*Dollars.*

I, ——— ———, [name of owner, shipper, or consignor], hereby certify that the above is a full and true statement of the kinds, quantities, and values, and destination of all the articles delivered by me for exportation as aforesaid.

——— ———,
Owner or Agent.

[Residence] ——— ———.
[Date] ——— ———, 19—.

Any owner or agent may include in a single manifest all articles exported by him on one train. (Customs Regs., 1899, art. 1887.)

9. The manifest of the owner, or of his agent, will be transmitted and delivered to the collector of customs at the last port in the United States through which such commodities pass into foreign territory, in such manner as the exporter may elect; but to obviate delay at the frontier port, it is recommended that the manifest be intrusted to the railway or transportation company, to be carried along with the goods and delivered by such company with the car manifest which said company is also required to deliver to the collector of customs at the frontier port before the goods can pass into the foreign territory.

Care should be taken by exporters and railway companies that the shipper's and car manifests provided by sections 1887 and 1891 shall be left at the last point in the United States whence the merchandise finally passes into adjacent territory for export. For instance, the shipper's and car manifests of domestic merchandise which leaves the United States at Sault Ste. Marie, Detroit, or Port Huron, passes through Canada, reenters the United States at Lowelltown, Me., and is finally exported through Vanceboro in the customs district of Bangor, Me., should not be delivered up at the first point of departure from the United States into Canada, but the merchandise should be listed as for export via Vanceboro, and the shipper's and car manifests above indicated should be invariably retained and delivered up to the customs officer at Vanceboro, and not at the first point of crossing from the United States into Canada en route through Vanceboro. This regulation applies to much of the east-bound exports over the Canadian Pacific and Grand Trunk railroads, as well as to others when like conditions attend the traffic. (Customs Regs., 1899, art. 1888.)

10. The manifests of owners or shippers of goods to be exported, intrusted to railway and transportation companies and collectors of customs, should be treated as confidential, and their contents should not be disclosed to outside parties without the consent of the Government, and then not in such manner as to disclose the business of individuals. (Customs Regs., 1899, art. 1889.)

11. The law further provides that no railway car containing commodities the product or manufacture of the United States, or foreign goods, duty paid or free of duty, intended to be exported to any foreign country, shall be permitted hereafter to leave the United States until the agent of the railway or transportation company, or person having such car in charge, shall deliver to the customs officer at the last port of the United States through which the commodities pass into foreign

territory a manifest thereof, which shall specify the kinds and quantities of the commodities in the form prescribed by the Secretary of the Treasury. (Customs Regs., 1899, art. 1890.) One car manifest is sufficient for any number of cars in the same train, containing the same commodity and consigned to the same person, firm, or company. (Treasury Synopsis of Decisions, 15502.)

12. The car manifest which the railway or transportation company is required to deliver to the customs officer must exhibit the marks, numbers, description, and quantities of the goods corresponding to those contained in the manifest thereof furnished by the person exporting the goods, or his agent, but is not required to show their values; and shall be in the following form:

[Form No. 209, Customs Regs., 1899.]

CAR MANIFEST OF ARTICLES EXPORTED BY RAILWAY.

List, or manifest, of articles of domestic production or manufacture, and of foreign articles free of duty or duty paid, laden on board car (or cars) No. ——, (or Nos.) to be transported by the —————— railway (or —————— transportation company) to Canada (or Mexico) via (name of port on the frontier where the goods pass into foreign territory).

Marks and numbers of packages.	Description of articles.	Domestic articles.	Foreign articles, free of duty or duty paid.
		Quantities.	Quantities.

I, ———— ————, [name of agent or employé of the railway or transportation company], certify that the above is a true statement of the kinds and quantities of all the articles of domestic product or manufacture, and foreign articles, duty paid or free of duty, laden on car (or cars) No. ——, (or Nos.) for transportation and exportation to —————— [name of country to which destined].

[Place or station of agent] ———— ————.
[Date] ———— ————, 190–.

———— ————,
Agent or employé of railway or transportation company.

(Customs Regs., 1899, art. 1801.)

13. The collector of the customs district through which the commodities to be exported finally pass into foreign territory will detain at the frontier port any railway car containing such commodities until the manifest of the railway or transportation company, prescribed in article 6, is delivered to him; and until the manifest, exhibiting the kinds, quantities, and values of the several commodities, shall have been delivered to said collector, by the person exporting such commodities, or by his agent; or the information required by article 9, satisfactory to such customs officer is furnished him as to the kinds, quantities, and values of the domestic, and foreign free or duty-paid commodities laden on such car. (Customs Regs., 1899, art. 1892.)

14. The agent or employé of any transportation company who shall transport such commodities into a foreign country before the delivery to the collector of customs of the manifests, or information, as above

required will be liable to a penalty of fifty dollars ($50) for each offense. (Customs Regs., 1899, art 1893.)

15. The information satisfactory to the customs officer of the contents of the car, required by law to be furnished him, in case the manifests of the owners, shippers, or consignors of the articles, for good reason shown, are not delivered to the collector of customs as provided by article 8, will be a manifest or list of the articles laden on the car for export, which must show the kinds, quantities, and values of the articles and their destination, made up as accurately as possible by the railway or transportation company transporting the same, from an examination of the contents of the car by an officer of the customs and of said railway or transportation company. (Customs Regs., 1899, art. 1894.)

16. The law further declares that its provisions shall apply to commodities transported to the frontier in railway cars for exportation and transshipment to adjacent foreign territory in ferryboats or vehicles, so far as to require the person in charge thereof to furnish to the collector of customs of the frontier port information of the kinds, quantities, and values of such commodities. (Customs Regs., 1894, art. 1895.)

17. The form of the manifest to be delivered to the collector of customs by the person in charge of such vehicle or ferryboat shall be as follows:

[Form No. 210, Customs Regs., 1899.]

MANIFEST OF ARTICLES EXPORTED IN VEHICLES OR FERRYBOATS.

List, or manifest, of articles of domestic production or manufacture, and of foreign articles free of duty or duty paid, intended to be exported to (place of intended destination in foreign country) in (state whether in vehicle or ferryboat, and if in the latter, give name).

Marks and numbers of packages.	Description of articles.	Domestic articles.		Foreign articles, free of duty or duty paid.	
		Quantities.	Values.	Quantities.	Values.
			Dollars.		Dollars.

I, ——— [name of person in charge of vehicle or ferryboat], certify that the above is a full and true statement of the kinds, quantities, and values, and destination of all the articles in my charge for exportation as aforesaid.
——— ———,
[Place] ——— ———. *In charge.*
[Date] ——— ———, 190–.

(Customs Regs., 1899, art. 1896.)

18. Any vehicle or ferryboat on which such goods are laden for export will be detained by the customs officer at the frontier port of the United States until the person in charge thereof shall furnish the customs officer such manifest, and said person will be liable to the penalty of fifty dollars ($50) for each offense if he removes the goods to foreign territory before complying with the terms of the law. (Customs Regs., 1899, art. 1897.)

19. Masters of ferryboats or vessels required by preexisting law to

clear their vessel and deliver to the collector of the port whence they depart for the foreign country a manifest of the kinds, quantities, and values of the goods laden thereon for exportation, are exempted from the requirements of the above law relating to exports by railways. (Customs Regs., 1899, art. 1898.)

20. Manifests of personal effects or baggage of travelers carried on passenger trains en route to Canada or Mexico are not required to be delivered to the collector of customs at the border port when such effects or baggage are for the use of such travelers and not for sale. (Customs Regs., 1899, art. 1899.)

21. Manifests of merchandise shipped from an interior point in the United States for export from a seaboard port of the United States, are not required to be delivered to the collector of customs at the border port where the transportation of the merchandise is partly through Canada or Mexico, the statistics of exports in such case being secured at the port of export under a preexisting law [R. S. 337], relating to exports by vessels. (Customs Regs., 1899, art. 1900.)

22. In the case of express companies carrying goods from this country into Canada or Mexico, the agent of the express company may act as agent of the exporter and furnish, besides the car manifest, the manifest required by article 2, including in the latter manifest all the articles carried by the express company on a single train, taking care to enumerate the various articles exported with details as to kinds, quantities, and values. (Customs Regs., 1899, art. 1901.)

23. The car manifest provided by article 6 may be prepared by the railway or transportation company at any point which may be deemed most convenient. (Customs Regs., 1899, art. 1902.)

24. Goods shipped from the United States through Canada or Mexico for a market beyond those countries should be declared as for export to the country of destination and not to Canada or Mexico. (Customs Regs., 1899, art. 1903.)

GENERAL REGULATIONS.

25. All articles exported shall be valued at their actual cost, or the values which they may truly bear at the time of exportation in the ports of the United States from which they are exported.

26. The accounts of the commerce of the United States with foreign countries shall comprehend and include, in tabular form, the quantity, by weight or measure, as well as the amount of value of the various articles of foreign commerce, whether dutiable or otherwise. * * * (Revised Statutes, 336.)

27. Collectors will make a preliminary examination of all * * * export manifests of merchandise, and when found inaccurate or incomplete, either in the description of articles or in omitting proper quantities or values, or for any error apparent on the face of the * * * manifest, will require the correction thereof before * * * granting

a clearance. In the case of those lines of steamers sailing under special regulations, with a view to avoid detention and to facilitate their business generally, collectors will see that correct manifests of the cargoes they take shall be lodged at the custom house within four days after the clearance of the vessel. (Customs Regs., 1899, art. 1904.)

28. For statistical purposes, * * * the date of clearance will be regarded as the date of exportation of merchandise. (Customs Regs., 1899, art. 1905.)

29. Export manifests must be verified by the oath or affirmation of the owner, shipper, or consignor, in person or by a duly constituted and capable agent.

30. Care should be taken to report on the export manifests the foreign goods, duty free or which have paid duty, separately from goods of domestic product. In distinguishing between foreign and domestic goods, only those goods will be reported as foreign which have undergone no change in form or condition or enhancement in value by the application of labor in the United States. Articles made from foreign materials, or changed from the condition in which they were when imported, by repacking, grinding, etc., will be classed as of domestic product or manufacture. (Customs Regs., 1899, art. 1906.)

31. Agents of steamships, transportation companies, and others at points of shipment on the seaboard to whom is consigned merchandise on through bills of lading, or otherwise, from interior ports for export, should require the owner or shipper at the interior or initial point of shipment to accompany the merchandise with a list thereof or transmit by mail such list to the consignee or agent who is to clear the merchandise at the seaboard port for his information in preparing a proper manifest for the clearance of the goods. This list will show the kinds, quantities, values, and ultimate destination of the articles, inasmuch as the bills of lading do not contain sufficient information, especially with respect to manufactured articles, to enable the steamship agent or person charged with the preparation of the export manifest to intelligently comply with the law which requires such manifests to exhibit a full, just, and true account of the quantities and values of the merchandise exported at the port and time of exportation. (See paragraphs 6 and 7.)

32. The country to which merchandise is reported as exported should be the country to which it is destined for a market.

If the country of ultimate destination of the commodities is different from that for which the vessel or car clears or departs, collectors will require exporters or their agents to state in export manifests, as the country for which the commodities are cleared, the country of ultimate destination, or for which the commodities are destined for a market.

The strict enforcement of this regulation is especially enjoined with respect to articles of breadstuffs, provisions, and other merchandise shipped through northern border ports and Canada destined for Europe via Montreal, Quebec, and the St. Lawrence River. These articles are frequently declared by shippers in their manifests as for export to the Provinces of Quebec and Ontario when they should be declared as for export to the country of true destination in Europe, etc., beyond Canada, the shipment through Canada being merely an incident in their transportation to the true point of export or market. (Customs Regs., 1899, art. 1909.)

33. Collectors of customs shall report without delay to the nearest United States district attorney and to the Secretary of the Treasury all violations of the provisions of the statistical laws and will take measures in the usual manner for the enforcement of the penalty prescribed by the statutes for their violation. See prescribed penalties in paragraphs 4 and 5. (Customs Regs., 1899, art. 1910.)

34. In the expression of quantities and values in returns, * * * the fraction of the dollar less than fifty cents will be rejected, and those of fifty cents or upwards will be counted as one dollar. A like rule will apply to fractions of weight and measure. (Customs Regs., 1899, art. 1911.)

35. Statements upon the required forms, except of imports for consumption, Catalogue No. 292, must be mailed to the Bureau of Statistics from the port of New York within fifteen days; from the ports of Boston, Philadelphia, Baltimore, New Orleans, Chicago, San Francisco, and El Paso, within twelve days; from Galveston, Tex., within eight days, and from all other ports within six days after the close of the period to which such statements relate. All returns should be forwarded as much earlier than the maximum time here allowed as practicable, thus increasing the value of the statistics by their earlier publication.

To avoid the delay incident to awaiting reports of transactions from distant outports, collectors of customs on the Canadian and Mexican frontiers will include in their monthly statistical reports made to the Bureau of Statistics the transactions which reach them from the outports between the first and last days of the month, but officers in charge of outports will be required to report transactions to the head office of the district as promptly as possible. (Customs Regs., 1899, art. 1913.)

O. L. SPAULDING, *Acting Secretary.*

SCHEDULE B.

Schedule exhibiting the classification prescribed for monthly statements of commodities, the growth, produce, and manufacture of the United States, exported to foreign countries, required to be rendered to the Bureau of Statistics by collectors of customs.

No. of class.	Classes of commodities.	Unit of quantity.
	MERCHANDISE.	
	Agricultural implements:	
1	Mowers and reapers, and parts of	
2	Plows and cultivators, and parts of	
3	All other, and parts of	
4	Aluminum, and manufactures of	
	Animals:	
5	Cattle	No.
6	Hogs	No.
7	Horses	No.
8	Mules	No.
9	Sheep	No.
10	All other, including fowls	
11	Art works: Paintings and statuary	
12	Bark, and extract of, for tanning	
13	Beeswax	Lb.
	Blacking:	
14	Stove polish	
15	All other	
16	Bones, hoofs, horns, and horn tips, strips, and waste	
17	Books, maps, engravings, etchings, and other printed matter	
18	Brass, and manufactures of	
	Breadstuffs:	
19	Barley	Bush. (of 48 lbs.).
20	Bread and biscuit	Lb.
21	Buckwheat	Bush. (of 48 lbs.).
22	Corn	Bush. (of 56 lbs.).
23	Corn meal	Bbl. (of 196 lbs.).
24	Oats	Bush. (of 32 lbs.).
25	Oatmeal	Lb.
26	Rye	Bush. (of 56 lbs.).
27	Rye flour	Bbl. (of 196 lbs.).
28	Wheat	Bush. (of 60 lbs.).
29	Wheat flour	Bbl. (of 196 lbs.).
30	Preparations of, for table food	
	All other for animal feed—	
31	Bran, middlings, and mill feed	Ton (of 2,240 lbs.).
32	Dried grains and malt sprouts	Ton (of 2,240 lbs.).
33	Other	
	Bricks:	
34	Building	M.
35	Fire	
36	Broom corn	
37	Brooms and brushes	
38	Candles	Lb.
	Cars, carriages, other vehicles, and parts of:	
	Cars, passenger and freight, and parts of—	
39	For steam railways	
40	For other railways	
41	Cycles and parts of	
42	All other carriages, and parts of	

SCHEDULE B.—*Classification for monthly statements of domestic exports, etc.*—Continued.

No. of class.	Classes of commodities.	Unit of quantity.
	MERCHANDISE—Continued.	
43	Celluloid and manufactures of..................................	
44	Cement..	Bbl. *a* (of 300 lbs.).
	Chemicals, drugs, dyes, and medicines:	
45	Acids...	
46	Ashes, pot and pearl......................................	Lb.
47	Baking powder...	Lb.
48	Copper, sulphate of..	Lb.
49	Dyes and dyestuffs...	
50	Ginseng...	Lb.
51	Lime, acetate of...	Lb.
52	Medicines, patent or proprietary.......................	
53	Roots, herbs, and barks, not elsewhere specified....	
54	All other...	
55	Cider..	Gall.
	Clocks and watches:	
56	Clocks, and parts of..	
57	Watches, and parts of.....................................	
	Coal and coke:	
	Coal—	
58	Anthracite..	Ton (of 2,240 lbs.).
59	Bituminous..	Ton (of 2,240 lbs.).
60	Coke..	Ton (of 2,240 lbs.).
61	Coffee and cocoa, ground or prepared, and chocolate..........	
	Copper, and manufactures of:	
62	Ore..	Ton (of 2,240 lbs.).
63	Ingots, bars, plates, and old............................	Lb.
64	All other manufactures of................................	
65	Cork, manufactures of..	
	Cotton, and manufactures of:	
	Unmanufactured—	
66	Sea Island..	Bale and lb.
67	Upland and other..................................	Bale *b* and lb.
68	Waste..	Lb.
	Manufactures of:	
	Cloths—	
69	Colored..	Yard.
70	Uncolored.....................................	Yard.
71	Wearing apparel..................................	
72	Waste, cop and mill.............................	Lb.
73	All other...	
	Earthen, stone, and china ware:	
74	Earthen and stoneware..................................	
75	Chinaware..	
76	Eggs..	Doz.
77	Feathers...	
	Fertilizers:	
78	Phosphates, crude..	Ton (of 2,240 lbs.).
79	All other...	Ton (of 2,240 lbs.).
	Fibers, vegetable, and textile grasses, manufactures of:	
80	Bags..	
81	Cordage..	Lb.
82	Twine..	
83	All other..	

a Barrels or packages of different weights will be reduced to equivalent barrels of 300 pounds.
b Count each bale of weight below 300 pounds as a half bale and count 2 such bales as 1 bale for the return under class 67.

SCHEDULE B.—*Classification for monthly statements of domestic exports, etc.*—Continued.

No. of class.	Classes of commodities.	Unit of quantity.
	MERCHANDISE—Continued.	
	Fish:	
84	Fresh, other than salmon	Lb.
	Dried, smoked, or cured—	
85	Cod, haddock, hake, and pollock	Lb.
86	Herring	Lb.
87	All other	Lb.
	Pickled—	
88	Mackerel	Bbl. (of 200 lbs.).
89	All other	Bbl. (of 200 lbs.).
	Salmon—	
90	Canned	Lb.
91	All other, fresh or cured	
92	Canned fish, other than salmon and shellfish	
93	Caviare	
	Shellfish—	
94	Oysters	
95	All other	
96	All other fish and fish products	
	Fruits and nuts:	
97	Apples, dried	Lb.
98	Apples, green or ripe	Bbl.
99	Oranges	
100	Prunes	Lb.
101	Raisins	Lb.
102	All other, green, ripe, or dried	
	Fruits, preserved—	
103	Canned	
104	All other	
105	Nuts	
106	Furniture of metal	
107	Furs and fur skins	
	Glass and glassware:	
108	Window glass	
109	All other	
110	Glucose or grape sugar	Lb.
111	Glue	Lb.
112	Grease, grease scraps, and all soap stock	
	Gunpowder and other explosives:	
113	Gunpowder	Lb.
114	All other explosives	
115	Hair, and manufactures of	
116	Hay	Ton (of 2,240 lbs.).
117	Hides and skins, other than furs	Lb.
118	Honey	
119	Hops	Lb.
	India rubber, manufactures of:	
120	Belting, hose, and packing	
121	Boots and shoes	Pair.
122	All other	
123	India rubber, scrap and old	
	Ink:	
124	Printers'	
125	All other	
126	Instruments and apparatus for scientific purposes, including telegraph, telephone, and other electric	

SCHEDULE B.—*Classification for monthly statements of domestic exports, etc.*—Continued.

No. of class.	Classes of commodities.	Unit of quantity.
	MERCHANDISE—Continued.	
	Iron and steel, and manufactures of:	
127	Iron ore	Ton (of 2,240 lbs.).
	Pig iron—	
128	Ferro-manganese	Ton (of 2,240 lbs.).
129	All other	Ton (of 2,240 lbs.).
130	Scrap, and old, fit only for remanufacture	Ton (of 2,240 lbs.).
131	Bar iron	Lb.
	Bars or rods of steel—	
132	Wire rods	Lb.
133	All other	Lb.
134	Billets, ingots, and blooms	Ton (of 2,240 lbs.).
135	Hoop, band, and scroll	Lb.
	Rails for railways—	
136	Iron	Ton (of 2,240 lbs.).
137	Steel	Ton (of 2,240 lbs.).
	Sheets and plates—	
138	Iron	Lb.
139	Steel	Lb.
140	Tin plates, terne plates, and taggers' tin	Lb.
141	Structural iron and steel	Ton (of 2,240 lbs.).
142	Wire	Lb.
	Builders' hardware, saws, and tools—	
143	Locks, hinges, and other builders' hardware	
144	Saws	
145	Tools, not elsewhere specified	
146	Car wheels	No.
147	Castings, not elsewhere specified	
	Cutlery—	
148	Table	
149	All other	
150	Fire arms	
	Machinery, machines, and parts of—	
151	Cash registers	No.
152	Electrical	
153	Laundry machinery	
154	Metal working	
155	Printing presses and parts of	
156	Pumps and pumping machinery	
157	Sewing machines and parts of	
158	Shoe machinery	
	Steam engines and parts of—	
159	Fire	No.
160	Locomotive	No.
161	Stationary	No.
162	Boilers and parts of engines	
163	Typewriting machines and parts of	
164	All other	
	Nails and spikes—	
165	Cut	Lb.
166	Wire	Lb.
167	All other, including tacks	Lb.
168	Pipes and fittings	
169	Safes	No.
170	Scales and balances	
171	Stoves, ranges, and parts of	
172	All other manufactures of iron and steel	
	Jewelry, and manufactures of gold and silver:	
173	Jewelry	
174	All other manufactures of gold and silver	

SCHEDULE B.—*Classification for monthly statements of domestic exports, etc.*—Continued.

No. of class.	Classes of commodities.	Unit of quantity.
	MERCHANDISE—Continued.	
175	Lamps, chandeliers, and all other devices for illuminating purposes.	
	Lead, and manufactures of:	
176	Pigs, bars, and old	Lb.
177	Type	Lb.
178	All other manufactures of	
	Leather, and manufactures of:	
179	Sole leather	Lb.
	Upper leather—	
180	Kid, glazed	
181	Patent or enameled	
182	Splits, buff, grain, and all other upper	
183	All other leather	
	Manufactures of—	
184	Boots and shoes	Pair.
185	Harness and saddles	
186	All other	
187	Lime	Bbl. *a* (of 200 lbs.).
188	Malt	Bush. (of 34 lbs.).
	Malt liquors:	
189	In bottles	Doz. (qts. or their equivalent).
190	In other coverings	Gall.
	Marble and stone, and manufactures of:	
191	Unmanufactured	
	Manufactures of—	
192	Roofing slate	
193	All other	
194	Matches	
	Musical Instruments:	
195	Organs	No.
196	Pianofortes	No.
197	All other, and parts of	
	Naval stores:	
198	Rosin	Bbl. *b* (of 280 lbs.).
199	Tar	Bbl. *b* (of 280 lbs.).
200	Turpentine and pitch	Bbl. *b* (of 280 lbs.).
201	Turpentine, spirits of	Gall.
202	Nickel, nickel oxide, and matte	Lb.
203	Nursery stock	
	Oil cake and oil cake meal:	
204	Cotton seed	Lb.
205	Flaxseed or linseed	Lb.
	Oilcloths:	
206	For floors	
207	All other	
	Oils:	
	Animal—	
208	Fish	Gall.
209	Lard	Gall.
210	Whale	Gall.
211	All other	Gall.
212	Mineral, crude, including all natural oils, without regard to gravity	Gall.

a Barrels or packages of different weights will be reduced to equivalent barrels of 200 pounds.
b Barrels or packages of different weights will be reduced to equivalent barrels of 280 pounds.

SCHEDULE B.—*Classification for monthly statements of domestic exports, etc.*—Continued.

No. of class.	Classes of commodities.	Unit of quantity.
	MERCHANDISE—Continued.	
	Oils—*Continued.*	
	Mineral, refined or manufactured—	
213	Naphthas, including all lighter products of distillation	Gall.
214	Illuminating	Gall.
215	Lubricating and heavy paraffin oil	Gall.
216	Residuum, including tar, and all other, from which the light bodies have been distilled	Bbl. (of 42 galls.).
	Vegetable—	
217	Corn	Gall.
218	Cotton seed	Gall.
219	Linseed	Gall.
	Volatile or essential—	
220	Peppermint	Lb.
221	All other	
222	All other vegetable	
	Paints, pigments, and colors:	
223	Carbon black, gas black, and lampblack	
224	Zinc, oxide of	Lb.
225	All other	
	Paper and manufactures of:	
226	Paper hangings	
227	Printing paper	Lb.
228	Writing paper and envelopes	
229	All other	
230	**Paraffin and paraffin wax**	Lb.
231	**Perfumery and cosmetics**	
232	**Plated ware**	
	Provisions, comprising meat and dairy products:	
	Meat products—	
	Beef products—	
233	Beef, canned	Lb.
234	Beef, fresh	Lb.
235	Beef, salted or pickled	Lb.
236	Beef, other cured	Lb.
237	Tallow	Lb.
	Hog products—	
238	Bacon	Lb.
239	Hams	Lb.
240	Pork, canned	Lb.
241	Pork, fresh	Lb.
242	Pork, salted or pickled	Lb.
243	Lard	Lb.
244	Lard compounds, and substitutes for (cottolene, lardine, etc.)	Lb.
245	Mutton	Lb.
	Oleo and oleomargarine—	
246	Oleo, the oil	Lb.
247	Oleomargarine, imitation butter	Lb.
248	Poultry and game	
249	Sausage and sausage meats	Lb.
250	Sausage casings	
	All other meat products—	
251	Canned	
252	All other	
	Dairy products—	
253	Butter	Lb.
254	Cheese	Lb.
255	Milk	

SCHEDULE B.—*Classification for monthly statements of domestic exports, etc.*—Continued.

No. of class.	Classes of commodities.	Unit of quantity.
	MERCHANDISE—Continued.	
256	Quicksilver	Lb.
257	Rice	Lb.
258	Rice bran, meal, and polish	Lb.
259	Salt	Lb.
	Seeds:	
260	Clover	Lb.
261	Cotton	Lb.
262	Flaxseed or linseed	Bush. (of 56 lbs.).
263	Timothy	Lb.
264	Other grass seeds	
265	All other	
266	Shells	
267	Silk, manufactures of	
	Soap:	
268	Toilet or fancy	
269	All other	Lb.
270	Spermaceti and spermaceti wax	Lb.
	Spirits, distilled:	
	Alcohol—	
271	Wood	Proof gall.
272	All other (including pure, neutral, or cologne spirits)	Proof gall.
273	Brandy	Proof gall.
274	Rum	Proof gall.
	Whisky—	
275	Bourbon	Proof gall.
276	Rye	Proof gall.
277	All other	Proof gall.
278	Starch	Lb.
279	Straw and palm leaf, manufactures of	
	Sugar and molasses:	
280	Molasses	Gall.
281	Sirup	Gall.
282	Sugar, brown	Lb.
283	Sugar, refined	Lb.
284	Candy and confectionery	
285	Tin, manufactures of	
	Tobacco, and manufactures of:	
	Unmanufactured—	
286	Leaf	Lb.
287	Stems and trimmings	Lb.
	Manufactures of—	
288	Cigars	M.
289	Cigarettes	M.
290	Plug	Lb.
291	All other	
292	Toys	
293	Trunks, valises, and traveling bags	
294	Varnish	Gall.
	Vegetables:	
295	Beans and pease	Bush. (of 60 lbs.).
296	Onions	Bush. (of 57 lbs.).
297	Potatoes a	Bush. (of 60 lbs.).
298	Vegetables, canned	
299	All other (including pickles and sauces)	

a Class sweet potatoes under class No. 299.

SCHEDULE B.—*Classification for monthly statements of domestic exports, etc.*—Continued.

No. of class.	Classes of commodities.	Unit of quantity.
	MERCHANDISE—Continued.	
	Vessels sold:	
300	Steamers	Ton.
301	Sailing vessels	Ton.
302	Vinegar	Gall.
303	Whalebone	Lb.
	Wine:	
304	In bottles	Doz. (qts. or their equivalent).
305	In other coverings	Gall.
	Wood, and manufactures of:	
	Timber, and unmanufactured wood—	
306	Sawed	M feet (board measure).
307	Hewn	Cubic foot.
308	Logs, and other	
	Lumber—	
309	Boards, deals, and planks	M feet (board measure).
310	Joists and scantling	M feet (board measure).
311	Shingles	M.
	Shooks—	
312	Box	
313	Other	No.
314	Staves	No.
315	Heading	
316	All other	
	Manufactures of—	
317	Doors, sash, and blinds	
318	Furniture not elsewhere specified	
319	Hogsheads and barrels, empty	
320	Trimmings, moldings, and other house finishings	
321	Wooden ware	
322	Wood pulp	Lb.
323	All other	
	Wool, and manufactures of:	
324	Wool, raw	Lb.
325	Carpets	Yard.
326	Dress goods	Yard.
327	Flannels and blankets	
328	Wearing apparel	
329	All other manufactures of	
	Zinc, and manufactures of:	
330	Ore	Ton (of 2,240 lbs.).
331	Pigs, bars, plates, and sheets	Lb.
332	Manufactures of	
333	All other articles	
	GOLD AND SILVER.	
	(To be returned on monthly statements No. 8a.)	
	Gold—	
1	In ore and base bullion	
2	Bullion refined	Oz.
3	Coin	
	Silver—	
4	In ore and base bullion	
5	Bullion refined	Oz.
6	Coin	

Printed by Libri Plureos GmbH in Hamburg,
Germany